LA CAUSA

Other Works by Gregg Barrios

Drama

Rancho Pancho (2009)

Poetry

Puro Rollo (1982)
Healthy Self (1979)
The Air-Conditioned Apollo (1979)

Praise for Gregg Barrios' Poetry

PURO ROLLO

"*Puro Rollo* gives me most of all a sense of community – through its conversations, its sense and settings. All of the above are specific to the Chicano community. Yet this collection goes beyond. It is spiritual history."

– **Tomás Rivera, author of** *And the Earth Did Not Swallow Him*

"What emerges is a remarkably succinct vision of the human condition that goes from the small details of dreary lives to an astonishing universal. If *Puro Rollo* were merely keen observations of the Chicano lifestyle... Barrios would have contributed a time capsule depiction to the literature of American regionalism. But it is much more."

– **Alexis Gonzales,** *San Antonio Express-News*

"Barrios is entering into another world — a world which most Chicano activist artists / poets seldom had the luxury to explore: *el mundo de los sueños personales,* those personal labyrinths of life which eluded activist poets, for poetry could only mean continuous struggle to Chicano poets just a few, short years ago. Poetry now also means reflection on our human condition, as well as creative experimentation."

– **Ricardo Sánchez, poet, author of** *Hechizo/Spells*

"Gregg Barrios, the poet of the common man, gives us through authentic and well-selected images the essence of life in the barrio, in the community."

– **Luis Leal,** *La Opinión*

HEALTHY SELF

"If poetry is to be brought to life, it must become part of our life; for the greatest artist is he who experiences what is felt and understood by everyone. Barrios has risen higher by writing poetry that is at once clear, plain and straight forward."

– **Gerard Malanga, poet and photographer**

THE AIR-CONDITIONED APOLLO

"These are love poems: effectively splitting words up so that like a smashed kaleidoscope one word fragments into others, each evoking a mirror-facing-another-mirror spectrum of images."

– **John Rechy, author of** *City of Night*

LA CAUSA

poems by

Gregg Barrios

HANSEN PUBLISHING GROUP, LLC

La Causa copyright © 2010 by Gregg Barrios

La Causa is published by Hansen Publishing Group, LLC, 302 Ryders Lane, East Brunswick, NJ 08816

17 16 15 14 13 12 11 10   1 2 3 4 5 6

International Standard Book Number: 978-1-60182-500-1

Book design and typography by Jon Hansen

All rights reserved. Except for brief passages quoted in newspaper, magazine, radio or television reviews, no part of this book may be reproduced in any form or by any means, electronic or mechanical, including photocopying or recording, or by an information storage and retrieval system, without permission in writing from the publisher.

Hansen Publishing Group, LLC
302 Ryders Lane
East Brunswick, NJ 08816

http://hansenpublishing.com

Book web site
http://www.lacausapoems.com

to my father Gregorio Barrios, Sr.
photographer, raconteur y *cabrón*.

to Marilu Massignani
teacher, activist e *gramscista*.

to Merrell Frankel
teacher, feminist *und übermensch*.

Home of lost causes, and forsaken beliefs, and unpopular names, and impossible loyalties!

— **Matthew Arnold**

Contents

Foreword xiii
Acknowledgements xv

LA CAUSA

The Searchers 3
Border Radio 4
Birthmark 6
Occupied Territories: A Diptych 7
Carnales 9
Salton Sea 10
Magic Shrooms 11
Crystal Heirloom 12
El Mono Loco at 34 13
Siempre, Fidel 16
T*H*E F*L*O*W*E*R T*H*I*E*F 17
Go West 20

~~LA CAUSA~~

Poema 25
Sin Lucio 27

L.A. CA. U.S.A.

Our Lady of Angels Has No Papers 47
Sunday Afternoon in Alameda Park 49
[His] Panic in Detroit 50
The Man in the Fog 59
Boulevard of Broken Noses 60
Gimme Shelter 64
Free Ramsey Now! 65
Coastal Highway 68
Homeboy [Sonnet] 69
Great César's Ghost 70
Remote Control 73

Sacrifice of the Sun Virgin 74
Waiting for the End 75
1984: Knockin' at Your Door 77
Please Don't Bury Me Alive 79

Notes 81
About the Author 84

FOREWORD

Gregg Barrios' latest collection of poems *La Causa* is the perfect counterpoint to his first book of poetry *Puro Rollo* (called by *the* Tómas Rivera "a spiritual history.") A fascinating interplay of the eras, voices, and regions of Aztlán, all in a simultaneous dialogue with each other, *La Causa* is an evolution in time, maturity, political sophistication, and expectation, a fifth dimension to the young voices in *Puro Rollo*, and an invaluable document to any artistic or historical study of the soul of *el movimiento*.

Internationally acclaimed as a playwright and journalist, Barrios has once again proven his literary weight – but this time in poetry. Barrios reflects both the pain and the pungency of the aftermath of the dream battlefield and the beauty and haunting purity of the idealism from which the dreams blossomed.

Each of the three sections carries its engaging esthetic. The clean innocence and naked tragedy of *La Causa* spreads across the Southwest and Mexico in tender, clean lines, compact and entrancing, understated, yet saying so very much.

The second section's crossed-out title La Causa carries implicitly the innovative boldness of the Chicano Movement, a time period when we dared to mix languages, create languages, invent new forms, rules, genres, and re-write our own definitions of self and surrounding. The form and format for this expression reflects the time period, yet goes beyond. Barrios employ this brilliant vehicle to define and capture the spirit of transitions, revolutions, dissatisfaction, and change.

The first poem in this section, also with a crossed-out title, and in Spanish, emphasizes that which is missing, and is followed by an even bolder innovation, a poem that is not a poem, a prose voice from the edges of the Chicano Movement, a revolutionary Mexican witnessing the visit of a media-seeking Chicano revolutionary and so much more, in a voice that is at once a negation of a tale, and the explanation of the tale itself. "Sin Lucio" breaks into a year-by-year narrative from the eyes of the revolutionary, and despite charging away from poetry right in the middle of the volume, transitions perfectly from the first to the third section, somehow explaining what has changed, what has happened, what has transformed and survived, despite being declared dead: this is how revolutions bloom, grow, then burst into "bullshit and living on the run" and finally reincarnate.

The third section, after *La Causa* has sprouted, been crossed out, and then re-surfaced as *L.A. CA. U.S.A.*, provides the coup de grâce. Even the titles feed us spiritually, despite the sadness and disappointment of that which a revolution finds as "leftovers" thirty years later. "Our Lady of Angels Has No Papers" draws on all the playful double entendres possible in this Spanish-English world, to let us know that even our highest deity, is one of us, *la gente sencilla, indocumentada*, without papers. "[His]Panic in Detroit" is another beautifully flowing, superbly crafted documentation of our modern Post-Chicano-Movement reality, giving us poetry, giving us meaning.

So what happened to the Revolution? Where did the Chicano Movement go? The final section of this book is thick with the correlations, facts, references, rhythms, lyrics and experiences of the time; answers to these questions; and, more importantly, answers to ALL questions related to hope and humanity, idealism, *el mundo cruel*, and the survival and *sencillez* of *gente honesta y activista*.

The ending poem "Please Don't Bury Me Alive" (another echo of the time period: the title of the first feature-length Chicano film) takes us back to Tejaztlán and Crystal City's spinach soul "as our future, our youth, fled our divided house.... no search for the spirit in the sky...a trip to el campo Santo today...the bodies had left, only spirits remain / bare faded markers, our ghostly past."

Barrios' work is reflective without sickening nostalgia, contemplative yet tenderly in the moment, and beautifully vivid: "The candle's caked wax a trail of tears / on my raised, clinched fist." For those who were there and wonder where it went, for those who weren't there and wished they'd seen it, and for those who are still in it, still pushing the placards and the boundaries forward, gracias, Gregg, for that still-raised, still-clinched fist.

Carmen Tafolla
San Antonio, Aztlán, 2010

Carmen Tafolla is a legendary force in Chicana/o poetry. Her work has been recognized as "giving voice to the peoples and cultures of this land." She received the Art of Peace Award for writing. Her prize-winning works include a new collection of short stories, *The Holy Tortilla and a Pot of Beans* that received the Tomás Rivera Book Award.

ACKNOWLEDGEMENTS

Grateful acknowledgment to the editors of the following publications where versions of the work herein first appeared: ¡*Latina! Magazine*, *ProFUN*, *Los Angeles Times*, *La Verdad*, *San Antonio Express-News*, *New Orleans Review*, *The Rag Blog*, *Dos Centavos*, *Lowrider*, *Xicano Poetry Daily*, *La Bloga*, and *Poets Responding to SB 1070*.

Mil gracias to Carmen Tafolla for her generosity and friendship, and for voicing those changes the Chicano renaissance wrought for our people, our literature and our culture.

Special thanks to the following people who have provided extensive comments on these poems: Ben Olguin, Grace Soto, Virginia Maese, Merrell Frankel, Kristen Naca, Francisco X. Alarcón, Steve Bennett, Ricardo Sánchez, Isela Vega, John Rechy, Ricardo Blanco, Alexis Gonzales, Danny De La Paz, Marian Haddad, and Gerard Malanga.

Additional thanks to The Harvard Graduate Creative Writing Program: Stratis Haviaras, and Gregory Nagy; NEH Fellowship, Boston College: John Tutino and John Womack, Jr.; Gemini Ink: Nan Cuba and Rosemary Catacalos; and to Sandra Cisneros and the Macondo Foundation for an Alfredo Cisneros del Moral Award and Fellowship.

These strengthened my resolve, allowed time to write, and affirmed a lifelong commitment to my art and craft.

I also acknowledge my publisher Jon and Jody Hansen for their generous time and energy devoted in transforming this manuscript into the printed word.

I offer a special *abrazo* to my buddy Mark Saiz and to my cardiologist Dr. I. Eko Tjahja for their life-saving efforts on my behalf. You made this volume possible.

LA CAUSA

You must explore your roots in the past in order to pinpoint your place in the present or to be entitled to a future.
— **Theodore Bikel**

Every view of the world that becomes extinct, every culture that disappears, diminishes a possibility of life.
— **Octavio Paz**

Yo quiero cuando me muera sin patria, pero sin amo,
tener en mi losa un ramo de flores — ¡y una bandera!
— José Martí

THE SEARCHERS

Like the wandering Jew
a man without a country
our lifelong search for
our ancient homeland

Aztlán torn asunder
divided, destroyed
beyond recognition
dream turned nightmare
plucked out by the roots
thrown to the winds

Yet signs of survival remain,
remnants here, artifacts there
hope that will someday burst
all barriers, boundries, borders

¡Aztlán! The word made flesh.

BORDER RADIO

"*La Pareja Ideal*"

churns in 4/4 time
on Radio Cañon
el locutor sells
whatever

"*con precios de 'me los llevo.'*"

24 hours a day
frontera sounds
blast away in
mountain time

"*las seis y nada en Juárez.*"

en la Salsa Restaurant
fajitas, cuatro tortillas
chicarrones con salsa
si paga más de $2.95

"*...está regalado...*"

boom box sound
on the highway
Los Thunderbolts
on Tex-Mex radio

"X-ROQ 80."

Little Joe's "Este Amor
Que Me Diste" secret
title as phones jingle
off the wall

"los mero-meros."

"Hola, Ana ¿de dónde?"
feedback fills the air
"baja el radio, por
favor, ¡ya gano!"

"La virgen de los zoquetes, ajua!"

¡Ay, Chihuahua,
hay nos vemos esta
noche en el Noa-Noa
a poco-poco-no!

"en la tumba descansamos!"

El Paso/Ciudad Juárez

BIRTHMARK

cloudy moon rises
over white silver
sands El Chuco
hills smooth concrete
loom like dunes awaiting
some pachuco's arrival
to mark in ancient script
name, neighborhood, street
magic marker popul-voh
a faded clue left to say
a 100 years from today:
Yo Soy, Yo Era, Yo Sigo. *

El Paso, Tejas.
"I am, I was, I continue to be."

OCCUPIED TERRITORIES: A DIPTYCH

RED ROCK

    Blackbirds cry
    across the desert
    dark clouds dip
    into Chiricahua Peak
    and Cochise Head
    where an 11-year war
    converted the Apache
    red-sleeved renegade
    avenging his nephew's
    death as vultures
    tear at carrion flesh
    red rock stained
    glass monument.

Ft. Bowie, Arizona

CALICHE

    clouds hang over
    the ashen mountain
    mesquite tumbleweed
    spotted arid landscape
    here the great Cochise
    once moved free
    dry lake bed filled
    caliche caked soil
    impervious to rainwater

residue glazed perfect
moment for a mirage
he walks tender foot
prints marked forever.

Cochise, Arizona

untie him and set him free
— John 11:1-45

CARNALES

    brothers in arms
    explorer scouts search
    party pass and nudge
    earthy quakers sitting
    down thee and thou
    walkman on water
    turquoise & silver
    borderline new mex
    music in 4/4 time
    uniform walk on dark
    glass observation deck
    banging drum sticks
    a muzak beat to wake
    Lazarus from the dead.

Raton, N.M.

SALTON SEA
After Bruegel's "Landscape with the Fall of Icarus"

Snake-winding sidewinder
From Yuma to Indio
Cochise's face appears
as a 4 x 4 whizzes by

blurring snow-capped
peaks plumed serpentine
clouds gazing sheep
peek as the Sunset

California Limited
crosses el río Colorado
crimson fuses into tan
acres aching native

Americans pluck
eye-filling oasis
camp site dock
'bago landlocked

mirage flickers on
water brown boy
dives into the lake
after a flying squirrel

only talapia notice
unabated, swim away

MAGIC SHROOMS

Maria Sabina wise mazatecan dead
and buried after a three day wake
in Sierra Huautla de Jiménez 550
kilometers southeast of la capital.

"I see my grandparents, my parents,"
last lucid words, last worldly verse.
"I see a peaceful world yet I am sad,"
her last gasp for fellow travelers.

Jagger, Lennon and Dylan sought
wisdom from her children of god,
tripping on shrooms, tasting colors
touching thoughts, hearing plants

smelling words before slipping
into darkness, her secrets intact.

Oaxaca, Mexico.

CRYSTAL HEIRLOOM

The dream was over, we'd lost our youth
we worked your fields, taught your truth
returned sleepwalkers to an old haunt
returned shadows pale and gaunt.

Faced by this spectre of *habeas corpus*
it fell on us, but it never was just us
bled and pleaded in your name
let no judge or jury convict or blame.

We freed your streets, we danced your beat
we praised your feats, we withstood defeat
tempted with loss as we grow old
stories of that political past retold.

Will they recall how we rang your bell
or forget our moment in history to tell?

EL MONO LOCO AT 34

Barrio traficante José Luis
long clipped indian locks
forehead sexy John Saxon
in *Unguarded Moment*.

Moving toward his hidden stash
when cops banged on the door
opened wide this time round
as handcuffs made it official.

His Miranda rights read
white shotgun wedding
lasting as long as the dim over
head light bulb in the back room.

To the dark head of soft hair bobbing
between his tanned arms and thighs
free of tattoos giving him head aching
as he shoved her down to do it again.

At the new city jail everything clanged
stainless steel footsteps echoed metallic
industrial lights swayed in his cell
glow worming his transfixed pupils.

Dreaming of another nightfall
shooting up under a full moon
pungent smell of skunk persued
by barrio perros choking him.

Standing at the gym urinal
a shy boy approached him:
How'd you like to taste it,
puto? Sweet aroma arose.

He awoke to take a piss in
the bowl's copper kettle priingin'
in his ears a raspy voice echoes
"Hey dude, you're el Mono Loco!"

"Judy" aka Julian in the next cell
Whatcha in for? Dressing like a bitch?
"I escaped from la pinta, mano!"
He zipped up. Why'd the punk do that?

Judy replied : "An operation,"
(probably from butt fuckin')
Whatever happened to Tizoc
vato in jr high who blew him?

"Dead. AIDS in the rottin' Big Apple.
Buried her last year. You knew her?"
We were in the same grade, I didn't
Finish hadda go up North he lied.

Above, the talisman spun narcotic
until Li'l Joey, his 13-year old kid
woke him as his stepbro, Eddie
bailed him out on a $500 bond.

Eddie drove Joe's '85 blue Ford van
Li'l Joey glanced at his father's legs
Joe didn't look at carnal o hijo once
home the bulb was still burning.

SIEMPRE, FIDEL

beloved warrior
living life
upside down
low on the floor
wings wept
outta sight body
open to the slings
and errors saints
bore their crosses
to martyr doom
as if physical pain
lead to heavenly
ascension, an assumption
i refuse to believe
even if body counts
of ten extended
to infinity.

> *He blossoms, and he withers like a flower,*
> *fleeting as a shadow, transient.*
> — Job 14:2

T*H*E F*L*O*W*E*R T*H*I*E*F

I beamed, a surrogate dad
as you arrived out of the blue
New York Sunday Times in hand
knocking at my door that night
filled with birds-of-a-feather
chatter we made until dawn.

Planning our annual pilgrimage
gay south-of-the-border caballeros
bound for exotic Mayan fleshpots.
I saw my own wild streak in you
Greek-bearing gifted exchange
student home on holiday in Tejas.

Xmas day getting high listening to
Cissy and Lala wailing, "Band on
the Run" to a stoned mariachi beat
overdosing on that year's gossip
eating your jefita's menudo feeling
life could really begin before forty.

When I took that sabbatical in '78
we spent our last new year together
Nuevo Laredo cantinas y congales
driving back dark snow clouds
my limo zoomed toward San Anto
for your midnite flight to Brooklyn.

Heights on the road retelling myths:
your boys-only graduation soirée
queen bee traipsing over snoring
drones abandoning a humble hive
"I'm only movin' on, vatos, in search
of better days, *hay te wacho...*"

"A New York native born and bred"
was your calling card and anthem
I moved to L.A. on long distance
you insisted that "I Will Survive"
was a mantra to gay city souls
who had braved the year alive.

The last time you returned home
we missed each other by hours
at the Crew, I punched a new air:
"I'm a victim of the very songs
I sing," as I left the popper-
perfumed bars for the streets.

I took my blood pressure today
130/90, a 65 pulse—still high
my Apresoline and Inderol
pale to the big chill of your hit
and run-on sentence - an elegiac
intimation of mortality?

Outside, now faded limo parked
its shocking blue paint oxidized
I sit on a carpet hippie-indio style
Kate Bush whispering, "we're
cloudbusting, Daddy!" (Who never
succumbed to temptation as we).

At 16, you lead a candlelit march
for fallen Chicano vatos in 'Nam.
"Long live la raza, but let's live too!"
Your words echoed in the freezing air
the candle's caked wax a trail of tears
on my raised, clinched fist.

GO WEST

there's a man inside
trying to break out
face against the pane

Chicago skyway toll
boy at a swimmin' hole
windmill under a bridge

ship by the lake
avoids a mistake
silo points to low

and ticky-tack houses
by the railroad track
just seem to go and go

I don't know why
a borderline is a
longer way to hoe

this once pretty city
is still a sight to see
Picasso, Calder and Miro

when I feel this way
I'm just counting days
for the kingdom come

and the Santa Fe train
on the rocking track
never brings me back

I've been so disappointed
down in Southern California
well, you know I almost died

when I spoke to my mother
she said "if I had my druthers
I'd rather you turn back"

in Texas I know
it takes a lot of soul
to just ignore the fact

that I don't belong
it won't be long
I hit the railroad track.

baking powder houses
aren't rising these days
going backwards by rail

in southern california
they always warn ya
never to look back

while scraps of steel
from a million wheels
keep burning up the track.

~~LA CAUSA~~

We're not short of movements proclaiming that a different world is possible, but unless we can coordinate them into an international movement, capitalism just laughs at all these little organizations.

— **José Saramago**

> Monolingualism is a curable disease.
> —Carlos Fuentes

POEMA
[a un amor que nunca llego hacer amiga]

nunca estaré feliz
pero hubo un momento
cuando yo te quería
entonces todo lo sentía
cuando eras toda mi vida
que ahora termino
en algo triste y gris.

nuestro amor iba comenzar
nuestra vida, ahora perdida
para que te voy a engañar
fui el cobarde en no decírtelo
siempre me hacías muy feliz
pero en vez de gritártelo
tome el papel de un infeliz.

nunca quise ser el solitario
¿por qué no me sacudiste con cariño
para matar el ladrón melancolía
que dejo estas cenizas de amor?
fui el único que te quiso
soy el único sin tu amor
viviré mi vida triste y gris

la paloma a mi corazón no aviso
solo fue la palabra que me condeno
ya ni besos pueden despertarme
ya no pido ningún perdón

ya no tengo nada de que olvidarme
porque solo estoy, solo estoy
sin ti, mi corazón.

> All I learned about guerrilla fighting came from Hemingway's For Whom the Bell Tolls.
> —Fidel Castro

SIN LUCIO
My years of living dangerously

1960 I was born on November 23, 1963, in Mexico, in the state of Guerrero, in the village of Tecpan de Galeana—located midway between Acapulco and Zihuantanejo. When I was seven—the year I made my first communion—I had already committed my first subversive act.

When I was just four, I had already learned the meaning of work. *"Tacos. Ricos Tacos de cabeza de res y chivo."* I'd shout atop a stack of wooden Coke cases in front of my family's makeshift taco stand. By family, I mean my abandoned mother who made the tacos and my grandfather who supervised the operation.

"That kid will be politician. Just wait and see," the men like old dogs would bark. "With his golden voice; he'll be a great singer." Women with shiny, clean braids of hair would tease.

When I was six, one of our regular customers, who ran a newspaper stand, offered me an afternoon job, hawking the daily newspaper from Acapulco—*La Verdad*—The Truth.

My mother was opposed. "He's too young. He hasn't learned to read or write." She, of course, hadn't either. Maybe she feared that she'd lose me like she had my father who had gone to el norte before I was born.

My grandfather added that when he was my age he was already fighting with Pancho Villa. Having a business—especially a taco stand—was a fruit of the revolution. "What honor is there in selling yesterday's news?"

Since I had the final say, I argued that the dealer could read that day's headline and that way I'd memorize it. Why couldn't I sell tacos in the morning and newspapers in the afternoon? Besides, we needed the extra money.

27

One day in 1969, an eight-column headline of *La Verdad* read: "CABALLERO ABURTO IS GOING TO FALL!" Well, on my rounds through the town's streets, I shouted up to the doors of the municipal palace—unaware that Caballero Aburto the governor of Guerrero was inside.

"Caballero Aburto is going to fall; it's in *La Verdad*." I pealed.

The governor came out into the street and bought all thirty copies I had at 20 times the usual one-centavo price.

When I got home I told my family. I expected them to be overjoyed. Instead my grandfather said that now the governor would send his men to watch him. "In the time of my general…" My mother was frightened and quickly said I had to confess what I had done. But I was barely six so I had to wait a year. Still they kept the money and never said another word. The next day my boss asked me for his cut. I told him it had only been a tip.

When I became seven—the age of reason—I was instructed by my mother and the church to make a formal confession before I could receive my first communion. That was why I confessed that transgression to God.

"What you did was involuntary, but subversive." The priest—Father Andrés—attempted to interrupt me.

I asked him, "I made money dishonestly. Hadn't I had robbed from a rich, important man?" I paused, terrified by the echoing silence. From the other side of the confession box, I heard Father Andrés chuckle. As he gave me absolution, he added, "Go in peace, my young revolutionary."

One hot afternoon after I started to make my rounds, I entered the medical building where I delivered a copy to Doctor Manuel Urrogete, an Acapulcan who served the wealthier families. Those who couldn't afford his services criticized him for his "city ways." Most of his patients were pregnant women.

As I moved up the stairs two steps at a time and counting, trying to best my record of reaching the third floor in a minute, a workman's horse blocked the second story stairs.

I glanced at the elevator, a small, slow, creaky device about to close and rushed in as the door shut.

Imagine my surprise to find that the two passengers in the elevator were my mother and grandfather.

"Mama, is anything wrong, who's watching the stand?"

She looked at me in a pale, almost fearful way that I seen once on her face when she had accidentally dropped a kettle of scalding water at my feet.

"I-It's your grandfather...he's not feeling well." I looked at my grandfather as the elevator stopped, but the door wouldn't open. It was stuck.

"Well? Nothing works as well as before, but certainly I'm in better shape than this Carranzista elevator." He banged his cane at the door.

"Victor, help me pray, that we are safely rescued from this device." She knelt, crossed herself and began to say her rosary. She was shaking.

"Victor, if you stand on my shoulders, you can get through the top of the roof." I laughed at my abuelo's suggestion. I was afraid that he could no longer support himself on his own legs much less with me standing on top of him. Instead, I used his cane and pushed open the ceiling trap door then shouted in my loudest street voice.

"Extra! Extra. *Una familia atrapada en ascensor.*"

I soon heard other voices echo above and below us. Suddenly, the elevator jerked open with such intensity that both my mother and grandfather fell to the floor.

29

Dr. Urrogete was standing at the door.

"Let me!" he said as I was helping my mother up.

"Lupe, did you hurt yourself? This could be bad."

"Oh, Victor, what are you doing here?" He asked as he recognized me.

"Bringing your newspaper. And this is my mother and grandfather."

It was then that my mother fainted.

1961 I had barely entered second grade the year cyclone Tara hit the Pacific coast. It destroyed the harvest, the bridge, the school, my house and the taco stand. It also ended my enterprising job.

We found refuge in nearby Coyuca de Benítez with relatives who had a roof over their heads. Somehow we managed to live from leftovers and hand-me-downs provided by the "good consciences" of the well-to-do that my relatives worked for.

I didn't return to school until I was eleven years old—when my godparents, prosperous hemp merchants, took me back to Tecpan and the reconstructed José Vasconcelos rural elementary school.

1967 By fourteen, I read the newspapers—daily. On May 18th, a small multitude gathered in the town square of Atoyac, a small village near Tecpan. It was there that Lucio Cabañas, an ex-teacher turned revolutionary, cautioned: "If they kill just one of us or even if they leave just one of us wounded, it will be the last time we try to do something peacefully. We'll take up arms and finish with those wealthy pigs. Long live the Poor People's Party!"

Some nearby officials took up the invitation and opened fire. In the shootout—later denied by the army—seven were killed. Lucio escaped that time, but he kept his promise and retreated into the Sierra Madre—his followers chanting: "Viva Lucio. Viva Lucio."

Since I could quickly memorize long passages, I came to the attention—again—of Padre Andrés Moreno, now, the pastor of La Señora de Dolores parish. As far as I could tell, he was more liberal than most in that village.

"Jesus was a true socialist," he declared one Saturday afternoon in catechism class. He often talked about Carlos Marx, Cervantes and Guillermo Shakespeare rather than Our Lady of Guadalupe or the saints. All us *chavalitos*—kids—eagerly soaked up his stories of doomed heroes fighting against oppressive windmills or czars.

He trained me to be an acolyte. *"Ad deum qui laetificat juventutem meam,"* I would recite in Latin. I thrilled at the secret language that Father Andres and I shared to speak directly to God. Some of the other chavos – puros indigenes were jealous and they'd taunt me in Nahuatl, the ancient dialect of the Aztecs. I only laughed when they asked if I was a Tarahumara.

More importantly, I was the cleric's assistant in caring for victims of altercations among the rebels.

One such rebel, César de Los Ángeles, then head of the Socialist Workers' Party—and recovering from a leg amputation—took an interest in my political education. He had me read—socialist propaganda—aloud to him. It gave him strength to endure his physical pain—and often put him into a deep slumber. Surprisingly, among the fodder, I found a gold mine in the writings of Ricardo Flores Magón.

I decided at that early age to model my life after Magón, a newspaper man, who formed the Mexican Liberal Party (PLM) during the Revolution. He had been the true voice of the revolution—only to be silenced by his forced exile—and prison death in the United States.

I became a first year student in a private religious school with a scholarship that Padre Moreno obtained for me. He must have known it was the right place for me.

1970 I was elected president of the student council in my second year at the Autonomous University of Guerrero. As a dorm counselor, I had few occasions to hitchhike home and be with my family.

Back home, the ever-present poverty, sickness now stuck in my craw. All that my grandfather fought for—the revolution, his children, and the taco stand—had faded into tequila-tinged ramblings.

Only my mother Guadalupe remained by his side and in his favor. What good was an education if it didn't put food on the table? Their silent stares and unspoken words accused me.

I coaxed them to the movies—recalled sitting on my mother's knee watching *Flor Silvestre* as my grandfather cried silently as the teacher tried to save a village. Those movies had inspired and united el pueblo.

Inside the aging Cinelandia, before the first film was over, my mother who had been watching me instead of the screen whispered.

"*M'jo me siento mal*—I feel bad."

Had it been the walk or the fact that next to the grandeur of Mexico's once golden age of films, these *churros* were nothing but silly cartoons?

Once Jorge Negrete's victorious grito sent shivers and a sense of collective pride. Once María Felix's sensual beauty elicited a collective gasp. Now all we had were second-rate comics and foul-mouthed singers.

Was Cabañas right? Was the only way to change the government by open rebellion and confrontation? Couldn't one be an intellectual like Magón and write stirring tracts? Yes, but despite their brilliance, who would read them? Wasn't his self-imposed exile—away from the people's struggle—a coward's way out?

Although I already enjoyed speaking in front of others, joining the university debating team wasn't just a means of defending or defining myself but a means of economic survival. Each time I won an oratorical contest I was excited in a way I had never felt before. I'd even receive cash prizes—up to three thousand pesos—when I placed first. The money I sent home was never acknowledged and I found myself further from my family.

When one of Cabañas's allies, Genaro Vázquez kidnapped our respected rector, Lic. Cayetano Díaz, the student body—although most sympathized with the rebels— was outraged. After that monstrous reality invaded our sheltered world of paper tigers and toy soldiers, none of us would remain the same.

1972 I reluctantly brought myself back home for my grandfather's funeral. I cried more for the miserable existence in my village than my grandfather's death or my mother's suffering—looking older than her years—still waiting for my father to rescue her—us.

Back in college, I now identified completely with the guerrillas—rationalizing in debates—much to the amazement of my schoolmates—that the rector's murder had been a justified act against the exploitative bourgeois class. In leftist student groups, such public acts of confession were a moral obligation—and rationalized without discussion. Yet, when we did discuss Marxist theory—in retrospect, sophomorically—we accepted it without considering the possibility that socialism might not work in Mexico.

If Lenin said: "The workers themselves cannot acquire the revolutionary conscience; it will come to them from outside transmitted by the intellectuals," we understood that our job as "Leninist intellectuals" was to undertake the organization of the pueblo into revolutionary cells dedicated to clandestine struggle.

To us no other destiny was—as Che had eloquently put it—"as noble as the rank of a guerrilla." When the opportunity to enlist in the rebel movement finally presented itself, I left for the Sierra Madre without a moment's thought or hesitation.

1973 The word was out. The Mexican resort owners publicly declared that our movement has damaged the tourist trade. We had scared the American tourists shitless—and they were taking their business elsewhere.

Ironically in the encampment I was assigned to—some 70 kilometers north of Acapulco—I had the *turistas*—the worst kind of dysentery. Around here, the joke was: if you can survive the shits, you don't fear death.

"El Pelón"—Baldy—Echeverría, the president of the republic, ordered the national army to ferret out *"ese pinche cabrón—* that fucking sonovabitch—Lucio Cabañas." El Pelón's advisors— American military experts fresh from the Vietnam War—told him that napalming the Sierra might be the best way of eradicating the problem.

We lived from booty obtained in our attacks and abductions. The rest of the money went into arms and ammunition. There were more converts and—naturally—more expenses and more assaults needed.

I quickly adapted to the routine—guarding prisoners or crops of marijuana with a M1 rifle and thirty rounds.

My wire-rimmed glasses were the only reminders of my former life.

The moustache and goatee I grew suited my thin, lithe body. I felt as my grandfather must have when he fought with Villa in the revolution. I also composed tracts in the name of the Poor People's Party.

Cabañas's directives often demanded freedom of political prisoners, millions of pesos for kidnapped officials, and more weapons. One demand was for the media to broadcast our communiqués and corridos. I eagerly recorded the communiqués— but bowed to the wishes of the leaders who felt that having TV and radio announcers read our demands would be a greater victory.

Brief—almost anonymous—relations with women were allowed. I found a *compañera* Miroslava, whose dark mestizo beauty echoed Dolores Del Rio in *María Candelaria*. She wanted to have my child. After all, she argued— in the throes of passion— a new life would remain if I were killed. Enflamed by her argument, I came inside her in long, slow ejaculations.

Back at the encampment, those moments were left behind. My—our abiding passion was *la causa*: the fellow comrades-in-arms with whom we lived, dreamed and struggled.

When I was twenty, I met Carmelo Cortés. A few years earlier, he had gone to the sierra with his small guerrilla group—FAR (Armed Revolutionary Forces)— and allied himself with Cabañas. Cortés' personality dazzled me from the first instant I laid eyes on him. His common street kid looks and stature (five feet with boots) belied his 33 years. As an orator he was irresistible.

When Cabañas was secretly hospitalized—even he wasn't immune to opportunistic diseases—for treatment of a serious parasitic infection— he didn't delegate his command to his men, but to Cortés and FAR—several kilometers to the political left of Cabañas—whom they considered a timid reformer.

Cortés our Mexican Castro wanted to extend guerrilla action through the entire country instead of confining it to the Sierra Madre in Guerrero. He chose me to be his assistant since I was ready to "harangue and persuade those whose faith often wavered."

Since I didn't have any prior record of criminal conviction, I could easily travel throughout the country. My mission was to meet dispersed groups in nearby states and to preach Carmelo's brand of revolution and ignite the fire in the name of Cabañas.

1975 Carmelo was a father figure for me. I became his faithful dog. In the space of a year, I was with him day and night. I only separated from his side once. It was then that they assassinated him in the parking lot of a Sears' store in Mexico, D.F., where he had gone to buy a pair of sunglasses. I tried to swallow the pain, but more bad news followed.

According to a military report, Lucio Cabañas fell mortally wounded in the region of El Otatal in Guerrero on the 30th of November 1974. At first I didn't believe it. They had previously reported his death—even printed death photos. But this time, my spirit sank as I saw the blowup of a Polaroid photo of a serene Cabañas taken in better times—an armed comrade at his side. The photo filled the front page of *La Alarma* for which I paid two pesos.

"A modern day Villa or Zapata?" A headline asked above a photo of Cabañas' face—clean-shaven in death. Rumors abounded: Had he been decapitated for the photo while his headless body had been buried in a mass grave with a dozen other followers? The tabloid suggested that El Pelón had employed half the Mexican Army to track and kill Cabañas in the surprise attack.

Fighting back bitter tears—first Che, then Carmelo and now Cabañas, I kept repeating, like a mantra, words from Che's diary: "wherever death surprises us, welcome it."

In March, the few leaders who escaped alive met with other splinter factions high in the mountains. They decided to put aside their weapons and disappear into the anonymity of the cities.

"Without Lucio," they said, "we feel incapable of continuing the work. We lack his political vision."

For those of us who elected to stay in the Sierra, the bitter truth quickly set in: the government was winning the battle. We were being annihilated physically—falling apart like rotting lumber.

Everyone wanted to be a leader—to form his or her group. Sadly, many of them became nothing more than common thugs paying only occasional lip service to Marxist rhetoric. This downfall became the upshot that we had foolishly reached. We had let ourselves be deceived as Cabañas had predicted, and now the revolution was over.

1976   It was a year of bullshit and living on the run. We were forced to fend for ourselves—thinking only of survival. And often, we formed alliances with those whom we normally wouldn't have trusted.

One such incident occurred a year after Cabañas' death. A *pocho*—a Chicano—entered our encampment to distribute weapons from the USA. He claimed to represent the Poor People's Party across the Río Bravo. But he was in it for his glory too. He brought a television crew—from NBC News—that filmed as he distributed weapons - but none of the medicinal supplies or provisions that we desperately needed.

He burned both the United States and Mexican flags for the cameras—calling for an America without borders or Yankee oppression. Didn't he understand it wasn't the gringos who were killing us—but our brothers, our government? As he spoke, he avoided focusing on us.

Later, the camera crew interviewed me. "El maestro Cabañas told us: 'the duty of a revolutionary is to make revolution.' But it never crossed our simple minds that revolution could be anything other than armed struggle," I said clearly—without stuttering or blinking at the strong light mounted on the camera. Neither the Chicano nor the hard-liners appreciated my comments.

I never heard if my 30-second commentary aired across the border. But, shortly afterward, I learned the pocho went into exile—in Paris where he runs a popular Mexican bistro.

1977   I was down on my luck. My fugitive life had marked me as a dead man in the eyes of the government.

Then, a friend of a friend of mine informed me that the flamboyant ex-senator Emilio Fogata was now governor of the state of Guerrero. I laughed—recalling how Cabañas had kidnapped Fogata for 25 million pesos ransom back in 1972. The senator had been freed upon payment, but most assumed his political career had been effectively terminated.

"Wouldn't you know it," my friend's friend added, "Fogata is freeing political prisoners *before* the federal government approves his amnesty law."

I finally relented and with sixteen other companions appeared before the governor at the municipal palace. After we presented our plea, he glared at me. It amazed him that I was such a kid.

"They'd told me that Victor Hugo Pérez Felan was a soulless radical, but you don't have that look." Fogata said slowly and calculatingly. "I've ordered the chief of police not to pursue you any longer. You may go in peace." He then handed me his personal business card. "Just in case," he added.

Actually, he wanted to grasp the mentality of a guerrilla and he asked us to visit him. We became his laboratory experiments. This hard-nosed man—abducted and accused of being a reactionary by Cabañas—was giving the nation a lesson in practical politics.

1985 At 32, I was finally free. I officially married. My woman Miroslava and I already had a little son Amado, but I hadn't dared risk appearing at a civil ceremony. Father Andrés—now fifty years old—blessed us when I returned home.

My beloved mother lived to see her grandson baptized on the day we were married. But months later, she was robbed and left for dead on her way to work—killed by glue-sniffing punks. Through god's mercy, she never regained consciousness.

Miroslava and my son now live in my small house in Tecpan. I reside one hundred kilometers southeast in Chilpancingo, the capital city of Guerrero—in one of Don Emilio's houses, with several of his assistants. I lack three years to finish my law degree.

Don Emilio has proven to be a god-sent benefactor. Whenever my car breaks down, I only have to ask him to lend me one of his. I no longer believe the road of violence will solve our problems. How could I have gone so astray in my youth?

1986 My second son was born without an esophagus or an anus. The doctors told my wife not to lose hope, but still we were devastated. I turned to my two pillars of strength: Father Moreno and Don Emilio Fogata. Both stressed the same thing: Faith—one in medicine and the other in miracles. I reluctantly had the boy baptized as Cristóbal.

My studies were forgotten. I had to find work to pay for operations our son required. Through an associate of Don Emilio's, I was introduced to a drug trafficker who proposed a risky—but lucrative—mission. It meant entering *gringolandia* where I was to deliver contraband into the Sierra Nevada in California. It was my first time in an airplane—and to fall from the sky in a parachute. I had no choice. My son had to have a chance to live. He had become my mission in life. My wife was pregnant again and we prayed for a healthy little girl.

1987 With the money I sent my wife, my son Cristóbal was operated on. Now he can eat and shit like any other boy. I broke a leg when I fell out of the plane, but that didn't stop me; after all, I've had experience as a revolutionary. I wound up in a hospital in a town with my name—Victorville. Had my father gotten this far north? After my recovery, I hustled the dealer into working full-time for his operation—moving merchandise into the Los Angeles area.

I now live in Oro Grande outside Victorville. When I do business in Los Angeles, I stay in Bell Flower with María del Pilar—a Cuban exile—who arrived here during the Marielitos boatlift.

She is a self-made woman. She left Cuba as Roberto a *transvesti* and arrived here as María del Pilar, a woman. If Mexican doctors created an asshole for my son—why shouldn't gringos convert a cock into a pussy?

As a child he—she—read *For Whom The Bell Tolls* and was delighted to find a character with his name: Robert Jordan. "I am the son of Roberto Jórdan and María," he announced. When he came out of the closet—he renamed himself after the two female leads in the film portrayed by Ingrid Bergman and Katina Paxinou.

"Bergman was like me—always the revolutionary woman—from Joan of Arc to Anastasia to Golda Meir. In real life she went from saint to whore in the eyes of the public. A woman with balls—like Santa Barbara—the patron saint of my country—who once was a man."

Then she added, "Paxinou was a Greek diva and so *macha* she smoked cigars—like María Felix does—ha! And braver than that faggot Fidel."

Oddly enough, with her blond hair and blue-eyes, she could easily pass for a *gringa*. In La Jaula de Estrellas cantina in Hollywood, she occasionally appears in a second rate floor show—as *Marilyn Monroe*—while her underage *mojados y maricones* work the crowd turning tricks and selling crack. Only when we're fucking do I occasionally see (the sexual fantasy momentarily stopping) the prison numbers tattooed on her inside lower lip.

I remain faithful to my Miroslava. Under the circumstances, Pilar helps me forget my problems and, yes, my loneliness. In many ways, we're alike—creating ourselves anew—like chameleons— for a greater cause. Socialist revolutions have only brought lies, corruption and oppression to Mexico, Cuba and Nicaragua. We both want to see our countries proud—and free—again.

Still, I'm no fool. Mexico has little chance of recovery—unless it bends over and becomes the 51st state. Unlike my second son, my country has an esophagus, but little to eat—a huge fucked asshole, but in need of a new one. The great tyrant Porfirio Díaz was right when he said, "Poor Mexico, so far from God, and so close to the United States."

1988 Through María del Pilar, I met an U.S. agent. He already knew about me. At our first meeting he said he'd seen that report on NBC News. "Even that spic who worked for us admitted you have charisma and—*muchos huevos*—a lot of balls."

He wants me to serve as a free-lance consultant. I'm to blend into a drug cartel in the Sierra that Caro Quintero—who ordered the death of DEA agent Enrique Camarena—abandoned when he entered jail.

"Your government knows that its profits will aid those who are fighting for democracy in Latin America."

"My prayers have been answered!" María del Pilar said, agreeing to the offer. She told the agent—an ex-marine—that her mother had been fucked by a "Lance Corporal Jordan stationed at Guantanamo Bay."

I wasn't as enthusiastic. Would I ever see my family again? Was this the upshot of my noble experiment?

"All revolutions in Latin America begin in the jungles." The agent privately buttonholed me over drinks. Recalling my youth in the jungles of Guerrero, I knew I had unfinished business. But what truly convinced me was his offer to pay me in dollars.

How could I refuse?

1989 I received the final briefing for my assignment. I am a small cipher in a far-reaching operation. No glory, no backup. If I get killed, there is no name or tattooed serial number to identify me. A mercenary is a soldier of fortune.

My duties will oblige me to return to Mexico with a new identity. My code name is Lucio. My new "wife," Ingrid Stevens aka María del Pilar Jordan, will be going with me. After she has infiltrated the system, she will be terminated: a suicide.

Last night we watched a video movie—starring Hemingway's granddaughter as a Playboy model. María del Pilar said that the actress had undergone breast surgery to do nude scenes in the film.

"Her tits didn't come out too bad—but mine are perfect," she said cupping hers. "I am Papa Hemingway's true Cuban granddaughter."

41

I received word that Miroslava has made me the father of a baby girl. Ever since Cristóbal's birth I feared it was something in my seed. Was it tainted? I didn't want her to bring another mutant child in the world. But she is deeply Catholic and for her birth control is a sin.

1990 "Dear Miroslava, I am glad that the girl looks like me—that she is physically perfect.

"Yet I am saddened over Don Emilio's death. What a shame this great man was never given the opportunity to serve his country in the way that lesser men have--men who never had the country's interest at heart but merely their self-interests.

"I am also distressed to learn that Father Moreno has been transferred to San Salvador. I never can repay all he did for my family and me. Though the situation in El Salvador is difficult, I know he can face anything. He was a father to me—much like Don Emilio.

"When I return, I won't be with you. You may hear that I am dead. Rest assured that it isn't true. I miss being without you."

1991 The announcement appeared in the local Spanish language newspaper *La Opinión*. "Victor Felan, a waiter at a Mexican restaurant, died after being robbed and stabbed at a bus stop in Bell Flower."

It also noted that I was an illegal but had recently applied for amnesty. The murder was attributed to a gang member on crack who was killed by the police before confessing.

The authorities will notify Miroslava. Secretly, she will know that I am somewhere—hiding behind a newspaper doing what I was born to do, what I must do. The life of a revolutionary's wife is sad. But we must have *Esperanza*—Hope—the name of our daughter.

As I walked to the post office to mail one final anonymous money order, I wondered if *La Verdad*—or the weekly in my hometown— would run my obituary. Would some newspaper boy shout the news of my untimely death? Would anyone remember? Or would the townsfolk just shake their heads and say, "*Así es la vida*—That's life!"

I still remember what Lucio—quoting some Marxist writer— once said. "If we don't speak out and try to correct the injustices in the world, we shall be condemned to the silence of history."

Strange, but Father Andres used to quote a similar line from "Hamlet" in catechism class: "The rest is silence."

I always add an "Amen" — everybody would laugh.

L.A. CA. U.S.A.

The ideal of a single civilization for everyone, implicit in the cult of progress and technique, impoverishes and mutilates us.

— **Octavio Paz**

Lost causes are the only ones worth fighting for.

— **Clarence Darrow**

Putting out fire with gasoline...
—David Bowie

OUR LADY OF ANGELS HAS NO PAPERS

her bronze skin makes her suspect
and hell, no green card as well
la migra began raids downtown
where raza works and plays
hide-and-seek a jale if you dare
blame ICE's Operation Jobs
a lame way to sanction mobs
bent on scaring workers away
only *coyotes* worked today.

I heard talk in the poolroom
about shakedowns at dawn
trabajadores arrived at the plants
as the perros swarmed like ants.
I wanted to runaway from LA
where gente strives to be brave
"Stay inside. You might be next!"
niños in school trying to stay cool
recite,*"hay plesha lichens to di flac"*.

La migra won't be fooled by Laker
mania running scared into churches
are empty today, barrio bakers gave
stale bolillos away to few buyers on
Broadway's tower of babel hushed
the end must be near abuelita said
el pueblo can't celebrate las fiestas
patrias if they're rounding up raza
in la plaza Dieciséis, ain't no way.

They're taking the madonna of angels away
man, she wasn't a legal resident, you see
they raided shelters, arrested protesters
our mother struggled and fought to be free
Watch it! She don't speak *inglés,* your way!
out over the clash, what's that she says?
"Know your rights, stand proud, don't bend!"
or was it -*"los rinches son pinches también"*?
no sé, but she wasn't jokin.' Amen.

SUNDAY AFTERNOON IN ALAMEDA PARK
después del gran terremoto en la capital

Navidad 1985

Red neon Xmas wreaths on Insurgentes y Reforma
shield the tourists' gaze from razed skyscrapers,
los muertos and the homeless in a makeshift tent
city - a rural campsite in the center of the park.

Niños like palomas nest in the Juárez monument
vendors sculpt miracles from mangoes and pineapples
fire-eaters spit flames of hunger, the air with fumes of hope
a Beethoven statue cloaked in revolutionary garb hums
its 'song of joy' as lovers embrace to touch the earth.

Año Nuevo 1986

Punkeros piss against the marble walls of Bellas Artes
as El Ballet celebrates a revolutionary *grito y danzón*
in the ephemeral city, PRI-bought poinsettias bleed
y Copa Mundial banners wave in the freezing night.

In the fallen Hotel del Prado facing *el parque central*
Diego Rivera's mural of a dream lies in rubble
behind street barriers its historical dream of glory
Mexico's patrimony turned nightmare chronicle,
its frieze of convulsive beauty out of sight.

> He will die / with one thousand masterpieces / hanging only from his mind.
> —Abelardo Delgado
> I wait silently for life / to begin again.
> —Rodolfo Gonzales

[HIS] PANIC IN DETROIT

1. Diego Rivera. Infant in the Bud of a Plant. 1932.

They came to Gringolandia during the Great Depression, Mexicans crossing borders legally - even if they were Marxists – and god forbid – atheists. But some thought why bring foreigners to Detroit the eighth wonder of the world when our native born, out-of-work artists were more than up to the challenge?

But Edsel Ford believed my father was the right man for the job. Perhaps they'd name a car after him: a Lincoln Rivera and one after my mother – The Frida Ford. His and her autos for the Latin American sophisticate.

But this was a depression and we shouldn't get our hopes up too high. But true to his word, Edsel [they later named a lemon after him] designed an original car for Mama. Papa had to settle for a coupe instead of the limo he desired.

My parents came to Detroit to create – to show that art knew no borders, no boundaries. The assembly line in Rouge, the plant in Dearborn imbued my father with the idea that the worker was the wheel that made the machinery function. Hadn't Marx been fascinated by technology? I am certain that this passion gave daddy a *pinche* hard-on.

My parents came to Detroit to procreate – an heir to their legacy, who's have the opportunity to be whatever he chose to be - a child to bring them closer.

A bus accident had left my mama unable to bear children or so los medicos en Mexico told her. The doctors at the Henry Ford Hospital believed otherwise: She could have a child if she would follow the obstetrician's orders to rest, eat well, rest, refrain from smoking and drinking, and more rest. They were hopeful, watchful, and certain that I would be a healthy baby – an American born to Mexicans – a Mexican American or as they say in Mexico – un estadounidense - but more often than not - un pocho.

If you've seen my father's painting – *Infant in the Bud of a Plant* – the spermatozoa has taken root in my mother's womb. I am the brown embryo perfectly formed and in a restful fetal position. The panel is part of the greater work *Detroit Industry*, that fecund period produced my father's – and especially my mother's – best work.

Diegüito, Diegüito! In the beginning, she'd whispered my name into my father's ear as he caressed her swollen belly, echoing: Diegüito, mi hijo. Both imagined as only artists can - their greatest collaborative work of art – a son.

2. *Frida Kahlo. Henry Ford Hospital (The Flying Bed). 1932.*

Diegüito, Diegüito! Papa arises at dawn to make sketches of factory workers, mother starts her day at noon with coffee and cigarettes. She doesn't want to be cooped up in that hot apartment when she can be outside feeling the breeze near the Great Lakes gaining inspiration or whatever it is that artists do.

She is learning to drive a standard shift car. She must learn everything: when to step on the brakes, shift from first to second, when to let go of the clutch, and how to step on the gas without crashing. She abhors the mechanical. She complains bitterly, but it isn't enough to keep her from stopping.

At times she holds her belly and sing lullabies - *"la víbora de la mar, de la mar"* or *"El juego de Juan Pirulero"* - to soothe me. More often she curses a blue streak driving through downtown Motor City, honking her horn, cursing in her newfound English, "You shit sonovabitch, the light is green." But then one hot June afternoon, she suddenly applied the brakes and screamed. The jolt rattled me; for weeks I couldn't think straight. I couldn't think at all. Nada.

3. Frida Kahlo. The Abortion. 1932.

The bleeding started. She consulted her dear and glorious physician in la capital – "Should I hold on or abort? I'm too young to die." Ditto my exact sentiments. Weren't abortions illegal in the United States? The doctors in Detroit said bleeding is normal. She could carry me until delivery and then have a caesarian section - *From my mother's womb untimely ripp'd and not of woman born?* Shakespeare! It frightened the daylights out of me, but the bleeding stops.

Mama returns to partying. Feeling her oats, she calls old man Ford an anti-Semite. Papa is furious with her. Mama gets upset, and they argue loudly into the night. I begin to kick and scream for them to stop, gasping for air.

On the 4th of July, the bleeding started anew. I lose consciousness. My father rushes Mama to the hospital. *Veni, vidi, vientro.* I emerge from the birth canal stillborn – if you look at her painting *Henry Ford Hospital*, there is a rendering torn from *Gray's Anatomy*: Mother lies bleeding from her uterus, a horrific crime scene from Police Gazette or a grotesque etching by Guadalupe Posada.

In my mother's painting, six ribbons issue from her body as she lies in a hospital bed; one from her womb connects to a clinical study of a brown, full-termed embryo with male genitalia – that's me – *Diegüito, el bien dotado.*

Later, the doctors diagnose that I disintegrated into a bloody mess. For days mother cried and for weeks my father tried to console her. Only after she is allowed access to paints and a tin canvas does she begin to recuperate. And yet, I still felt pieces of myself inside her body.

Her first post-partum painting was a *retablo* that usually commemorates a death or a near-death experience, a *deo gracias* for divine intervention. But I never could figure whether she was lamenting my demise or the fact that she would never have children. And yet if she had only rested, watched her diet, stopped with the candy – especially the caramelos, the drinks and the cigarettes perhaps I would still be alive. As far as the driving lessons, don't go there.

Talk about omens. Three weeks later, there was a midday solar eclipse. My parents and friends gathered on the rooftop of the Institute of Arts to watch the planetary event through smoked glass filters. I kept hallucinating about bloody sacrifices to a sun god high upon the pyramids. Mother was not amused, but Father was. She hemorrhaged again. This time all remnants of my existence left her body and I never felt her closeness again.

My parents came to Detroit to create and procreate. They succeeded in the former and failed in the latter. Or did they? Diegüito, Diegüito! Mi hijo.

4. *Frida Kahlo. My Birth. 1932.*

In utero, my leaving mother's womb becomes her rebirth. As for me, I was a Mexican stillborn in the USA, *el nuevo hombre*, a Mestizo, a Communist, a Mexican American, *un vendido*, un Americano, an illegal – no, I'd claim dual citizenship. I was a Motown native son, un hijo de Detroit, Michingón.

And yet, I could have been César Chávez in the fields, Julio César Chávez in the ring, a rocket scientist, a pediatrician, a Detroit Tiger, Mitch Ryder and the Detroit Wheels, Iggy Pop, the MC5, Madonna, Kid Rock – even the real Slim Shady.

5. *Diego Rivera, Vaccination (The Holy Family) 1933.*

The most controversial panel of *Detroit Industry* depicts a child receiving a vaccination against the diseases that until advances in modern medicine were the scourge of mankind. I stand glowing like the Lindbergh baby. Mother is the nurse and holds me as a physician – my father administers the inoculation. I feel no pain.

The wise three behind us are medical scientists, bearing life-saving gifts. In the foreground, an ox and lamb provide serum. It is the first and only portrait of my family – the face of an immigrant familia in the 20th century – happy at last with a healthy, newborn child.

When the final panel of *Detroit Industry* was finished, I remained in limbo. The Rivera Court at the Institute became a monument, a crypt, a tomb to the unknown son, a temple dedicated to a Mexican master in the heart of the U.S.A.

Exactly nine months after arriving in Detroit, my parents fled to New York City for an ill-fated commission – a mural in Rockefeller Center. They never returned. Now, it was my turn to cry. I tried scream therapy like John and Yoko: "Mama don't go; papa come home!" I yelled my lungs out.

In la capital the bohemians marveled at the pickled embryo Mama kept in a jar by the door of her bedroom – a gift from her physician – but don't draw the wrong conclusion. It's not me – it doesn't have my DNA. My eccentric mother celebrated *Dia de los Muertos*, 24/7. And my womanizing father already had a string of *mocosos* from Paris to Monterrey. Go figure.

6. Frida Kahlo. *Self-Portrait on the Borderline Between Mexico and the United States. 1932.*

I can't recall the exact number of paintings my mother finished in Detroit, for they now reside far away in the homes of wealthy collectors. I was hopeful when the Tate in London exhibited "My Birth." I thrilled that its owner was a former Detroit resident, Maria Louisa Ciccone aka Madonna. Perhaps the Institute would impose on her largesse to mount an exhibit of Mama's paintings from that year of magical inspiration.

But I mustn't get my hopes up. We're in the middle of another depression in Detroit. I have to make do with the postcards in the DIA gift shop. If you're ever in the 313, look me up. My embryo fresco is the large panel on the left side portico above the information booth. The main panel of "The Holy Family" is straight ahead on the north wall.

My days are spent watching art patrons watching me both as embryo and holy child but somehow never connecting the pigments of time and space.

I'm studying Zen. The other day I meditated on a most enlightening koan: "Father die, mother die, this is good luck." Freaking heavy shit, verdad?

In the p.m., I look forward to the arrival of the lady security officer on the late shift - a Motown backup singer in another life - who hums righteous and soulful lullabies like "Hush, little baby, don't you cry" and 'Sometimes, I feel like a motherless child" until the boom box cacophony of the Mexican overnight crew erase that peaceful reverie with *narcocorridos* as they mop and buff the floors and set up for the next day's visitors. Most are unaware of my legacy or even who my parents were, but occasionally, I'll glimpse a younger one gazing at the murals in amazement: *"Watcha. ¡Que rollo!"*

THE MAN IN THE FOG

Last night in a dream
I cut my hair grey
dawn brought reality
to my brown indian

face in la madrugada
my deep roots of rural life
and Elvis Presley still alive
came back to haunt me.

My half-breed cousins
blue-eyed, blond-haired
left during the night
to a Nevada sunrise

Awake, in smoggy El Lay
Emmylou on the stereo
a dayglo C*H*A*K*A
tag outside shone brightly.

Santa Monica, Madre de San Agustín,
Reza por nuestros hijos de la Chingada.

BOULEVARD OF BROKEN NOSES

Hollywood 101 Freeway, Santa Monica Blvd Exit – Day One

Romeo thumbed a ride to L.A.
on a farm-to-market truck
man on a mission improbable
to be a Latino James Dean.

It's a long haul from Salinas
to selling fresh strawberries
by the basket, juicy oranges
by the bag on the exit ramp.

Glaring in the sun stripped
to his waist, body a glistening
La Raza billboard: UFW eagle
s-t-r-e-t-c-h-e-s pec-to-pec.

His sweaty back Technicolor
Virgen de Guadabuddha icon
with an emblazoned legend of
Viva La Causa, Viva La Raza.

From the corner of the freeway
the Hollywood sign a beacon
glowing white in the distance
a SUV arrests his attention.

For fresh berries, Romeo
hands him a basket but he
drives away without paying.
"Fucking wetback. Get a job."

Warner Bros. Hollywood, Santa Monica Blvd – a year later

Romeo moonwalks
an iPod beat robotic
ragtag costumed ghoul
fresh from a cattle call.

As a zombie extra he aced
two days of work at Warners.
He feels cocky and hard in black
studded jacket, latex surfer shorts.

Bare chest thumbing his shorts
down to his *aguila mexicana*
tattoo beak peeks on the bench
awaiting the number four bus.

Midday traffic halts hip soft
parade waiting for the light
his goatee smiles as a cougar
in a Cadillac offer him a lift.

Hollywood Hills, Los Feliz Blvd. – a month later

In the outdoor patio Romeo
gazes through his Ray-Bans
at his needle-damaged arm,
melting in the winter light.

The revolver in his pants heavy
he kisses his glow-in-the-dark
rosary to hex this day's death
from last night's crash and burn.

MacArthur Park – Wilshire Blvd. – six months later.

Romeo awoke before dawn confusing
the shelter for his jail cell touches his
bandaged broken nose, breathes deeply,
showers, gets coffee and walks outside.

MacArthur Park set of the Rescue Mission
PSA shoot alive with vendors of fake IDs,
fruit ices, kids on bikes, skateboards, moms
pushing strollers and dealers drugs.

His black jacket and bolo tie askew
with makeup and his bandaged nose,
his street preacher character apes Jack
Nicholson's noir role in *Chinatown*.

Action! He preaches the Beatitudes,
holds his Bible like an Oscar, vagrants
cast as the faithful fall as shots ring out
his Bible pierced, his young life saved.

Cut the director shouts. As Romeo awaits
the playback, an old wino approaches him,
"You remind me of a young James Dean."
Romeo smiles and signs the piece of paper.

>...ain't got no home, no direction known.
>—Clarence "Frogman" Henry

GIMME SHELTER

    the midnight mass of homeless
wanderers abandoned their tense city
witnesses to the black peace maker
lying dead, 33-years-old, 24/7
troubled sleep for Harry Rodgers
no bread and water hospital city
soup kitchen at 6th and Gladys
no miracles, only torn mattresses
empty refrigerator boxes, all that
remains of justiceville, a skid row
settlement in the shadow of Phil
harmonic hall dispersed a winter
night before death stole away
in his only pair of shoes.

FREE RAMSEY NOW!

When all is said and done
when you and I are dead,
your legend will remain
a true Chicano son.

It never was just us
it was you, me y todos
who believed our time
had come - and it had.

But politics is a fickle
whore who knocks on
every door for a quick
trip around the whirl.

You were the poster
boy for el movimiento
madres y palomilla all
voted La Raza Unida.

Ramsey for Governor
de Tejas was the rally
and the cry until they
put a spell on you.

We stood in disbelief
the gutless cynics
said you betrayed us
by not fighting back.

But where were we
when you received
a life sentence for
drug-trafficking?

Free Peltier, *simón que sí*.
Free Angela, right on, bro.
Free Ramsey Muñiz, and
the silence is deafening.

No solidarity or support
from those whose road
you paved, now elected
judges, mayors y mas.

Watching them on TV,
I wonder how and why
they lost their raza roots,
cut their native tongue.

I remembered the exiled
brothers Flores Magón
true architects and heroes
de la Revolución jailed.

A century later, you
occupy the same cell
at Leavenworth for a life
sentence of confinement.

We don't know how to
honor our leaders alive
only after they're dead
and buried en el olvido.

I saw a documentary on
PBS today a clip of your
vibrant face did express
real strength and grace.

Your voice had been erased
as if truth could cause riots
or upheaval in the realization
of how much we left undone.

When all is said and done
when you and I are dead,
your legend will remain
a true Chicano son.

COASTAL HIGHWAY

you are fifteen
you are fearful
on the highway
of the brave ones

coastal curve

la guerrillera advances
los soldados approach
nowhere to run
nowhere to hide

sharp turn

kill you if you will
kill you if you won't
aid the rebeldes
aid the contras

dead end

your brother gone north
your father taken south
watching for the turn
waiting for the end

HOMEBOY [SONNET]

never had a voice
much of a choice
on which side
of the border
line to decide
law and order

accept your fate
end up jail bait
for bigger fishes
to fight over
against wishes
to crossover

from this place
without a trace

> *I believed I was escaping from myself,*
> *but alas, I brought myself with me!*
> —Sor Juana Inés de la Cruz

GREAT CÉSAR'S GHOST

Salinas CA is east of Eden
In the land of Nod my Bible
teacher said and Steinbeck
wrote a novel by that name.

I never held a protest sign
walked the picket line or
worked the fields. I was born
ADD – Anno Domini Delano.

My folks fought and struggled
To give this land to us the meek
inheritors of the earth only end
betrayed by agribusiness greed.

I learned of civil rights
from the flatbed of a truck
heard Louie y los Lovers play
Omar the Gypsy wax poetic.

My first love was Mario
we made music and rhyme
he the music, I the words
our rich culture, our lives

Salinas is East of Eden or so
my teacher said, Steinbeck
brought dust bowl migrants
and a sad savior, Tom Joad.

But then reality stepped in
César organized the workers
the UFW brought better pay
the land of nod was a song.

East of Eden was just a film
Dean never made it here alive
and Wynken, Blynken & Nod
were just three men in a tub.

When the age of punk began
I put Baez and Dylan aside -
X was our Beatles – Los Plugz
and the Brat were our Stones.

I belted out, "Johnny hit-and-run
Pauline" like Exene with a mariachi
beat backed with the twist-and-shout
of Mario's funky surfer punk guitar.

Great César's Ghost!

Our motley band of outsiders
Mario left for L.A. I followed
a bitch in heat, loved him more
than me. He was my absurd vice.

We lived in the burnt-out,
riot-torn city of lost angels
cockroach street people never
landing a gig that paid the rent.

I sang siren songs for change.
Mario left me black and blue
S&M gay-for-pay, his habit
for a tweak and a H-nod.

El movimiento changed us
growing up I never knew
I'd lose myself to find me
exiled in the land of Odd.

REMOTE CONTROL

Dark green Palm Springs sun
hazy day away from East L.A.
chirping redbirds mock car
alarm aftershock response

Kids bound for home balance
ESL books on their heads
to be cool and well-read
instead of a dropout foo

Like gangsta Amado Guerrero,
now marching to a new beat
in El Califas National Guard
to fight a Latino Vietnam:

"I never expected to be home
sick by el Río Wawa in Honduras,
here I am - a Chicano Macho man!
sharing tokes, jokes and Bud Lites.

Stoned in this fog remembering
LOS homies bien calmados in
a Silver Lake palmado waiting
for a bang in the Valley smog."

SACRIFICE OF THE SUN VIRGIN

High above Mulholland
Las Alturas clouds frame
the backlot of Universal's
ancient pyramid set

You lie waiting in Chichen-Itza
rehearsing a blood sacrifice
Yma Sumac on the hi-fi
yucca-tanned tits hand-tied.

Tubes ignite the fire within
you lie wondering if the gods
will be appeased or if fire
mountain will grow angry

Since you probably aren't
what the director had in mind.

WAITING FOR THE END

celluloid credits roll
like mauve clouds across
your stunning countenance
crowds of extras roar out
fear gnaws your insides
as blood boils in theirs

wrong way no exit signs fade
into madrugada an angry mob's
darkest dreamscape projected
damsel in a distressing turn
sudden screen scream startles
director's pacemaker flickering

fresnel sealed beams focusing
French kiss in the graveyard
reaching out for the hairy hand
some leading man's trained double
take in disbelief as you turn over
in slow motion agony of reel death

at the edge of the abyss
the extras in death drag
await the end of the day
for night scene revealed
in a tarot game of chance
and little skill as an O

pal and Porsche race out
of control flaming car crash
in the style of an Almaraz
panoramic print of flying
wreckage on the highway
to heaven knows where.

Sauve qui peut la vie...

1984: KNOCKIN' AT YOUR DOOR

"Jump!" Edgar soberly said
was number one with a bullet
followed by "Cum Feel the Noize"
by Quiet Riot in the capital city

of his native E L S A L V A D O R
the day he left because of the war
"Edgar, *la tiene bien buenota*,"
a dazzling drag doll screamed

something he loves to hear
La Banda Tropical's *"Brujeria"*
blaring at La Jaula/The Cage Bar
en el mero corazón de Hollywood

its *Chilango* owner murdered
after a new year's lovers spat
now envious wags spread vile
rumors and bad news from home

a marine fucked his teenage sister
leaving her with VD and a bastard
half-black, half-salvatrucha like Fatso
who wants to make it with him later

"Qué viva, El Salvador!"
Edgar said half drunk, half hard
completely stoned, "Whatcha doing
tonight?" gulping, "whatever, mano."

the hostess in dragon lady drag
jangles her bracelets and waves
a telephone at Edgar dancing on
crowded floor of sweaty shadows

her wrist and elbow measure his cock
tales last call, "I'm not gay, but I need
to lose this," holding his Tecate beer
belly laughing as his machismo blurs

in the stranger's arms, wishing he were
home sober, aware the militia will
pick him up to protect wealthy brats
pretending that everything is cool

"If you didn't come to party, don't come
knockin' at my door," he mouths in lip
synch to music playing on the FM
over snores of tonight's old fart.

PLEASE DON'T BURY ME ALIVE

I sat by the banks of el rio Nueces
wept as I remembered our youth
how loud our talk, proud our walk
our realization que "si se puede!"

"It must be in the spinach,"
an aged adversary mumbled
his Del Monte can on the shelf
old order set out into greenwich

Turning on ourselves
a jab here, a jag there
as our future, our youth,
fled our divided house

Rather than fulfill the promise
a crossover dream, a nightmare
"I yam what I yam" — the upshot
of an ancient noble experiment

A kindergarten turned to symbolic weed
as hundreds of eager minds went hungry
Golden Chicken, Pizza Hut, Diary Queen
fast food, fast forward pass, fat chance!

Was equal opportunity all we received
because it was all we deserved?

No search for the spirit in the sky
no lofty goals to let us soar up high
no *caldo de res* just mom's apple pie
enough for Juárez to burst out and cry.

I took a trip to *el campo santo* today
the graveyard was tombstone grey
the bodies had left, only spirits remain
bare faded markers, our ghostly past.

I sat and spoke to el maestro Tomás
his father's name, his father's grave
the same, at his feet, I clutched earth
and it did not swallow me.

I reckon someday we'll meet again
recalling the poet's line, "*home is where
you go / when they have to take you in...*"
I was home for better or worse.

NOTES

The Searchers
Epigram is from Marti's *Versos Sencillos*. The title is after Tomas Rivera's *The Searchers and Other Poems*. Aztlán was the ancient homeland of the Aztecs.

Border Radio
X-ROQ-80 aka Radio Cañon gives listeners a taste of the music, flavor and dialect that transcends cultural divides. El Noa-Noa was a nightclub in Ciudad Juárez made famous by singer Juan Gabriel.

Birthmark
El Chuco — El Paso, the birthplace of the Pachuco.

Magic Shrooms — *for María Sabina*
Sabina was a healer and poet who attracted world famous rock stars to ingest her magic mushrooms –peyote.

Occupied Territories — poem for poets responding to SB1070.

Crystal Heirloom – *for Marilu Massignani*

El Mono Loco at 34 — *for José Luís Zapata Sánchez, RIP*
See also my poem "El Mono Loco" in *Puro Rollo*.

Siempre, Fidel — *for the Ayala Brothers de San Antonio*.
The title refers to the boxer's code: always true/faithful.

Flower Thief — *for Cleofas Tamez, RIP*.
The title from Ron Rice's underground film. "A Noo Yawk native born and bred," lyric from "Native New Yorker" by Odyssey. "I'm a victim of the very songs I sing," lyric from "Victim" by Candi Staton.

Go West — *for Willard Motley*.
Motley a black writer wrote about the down and out. Like Nelson Algren, he was a precursor of the Beats.

81

Poema — *para Alberto Aguilera* (aka Mexican singer-composer Juan Gabriel who refused to crossover into the English language music market.) The Fuentes quote prefaced his readings before a non-Spanish speaking audience.

Our Lady of Angels — *for Joan C. Baez.*
Epigram from Bowie's "Cat People." El Lay and LOS are used by Los Angelinos to refer to Los Angeles. *"Los rinches son pinches tambien"* translates as "The Rangers are also S.O.B.s"

Sunday Afternoon in Alameda Park — *for Carlos Monsiváis.*
"After the great earthquake in the capital" is a playful reference to Guadalupe Posada, the Mexican engraver whose images of horrific events were often reproduced in the dailies.

Diego Rivera's mural *A Dream of Sunday Afternoon in Alameda Park* chronicles the history of Mexico from its founding to the 20th century. The mural was thought destroyed in the 1985 earthquake. Years later, it was repaired and given its own museum in Alameda Park.

[His]Panic in Detroit — *for Eva Falcón Barrios – madre y mater dolorosa.*

The Man in the Fog
The title of the poem is taken from Gram Parsons' same-titled song - an attempt to blend norteño music with a country rock beat. Chaka was the legendary self-styled tagger whose infamy spread throughout Los Angeles County in the 1990s.

Boulevard of Broken Noses - *for John Rechy aka Johnny Rio.*

Gimme Shelter — *for R.R.R.*

Coastal Highway - *for Alex Amaya, Highland Park skater de San Salvador.*

Free Ramsey!
Ramsey Muñiz was the Raza Unida political party candidate for Governor of Texas. He was later convicted for drug trafficking and is serving a life sentence.

Great César's Ghost — *for Sandra Cisneros.*

Sacrifice of the Sun Virgin — *in memory of Maria Montez.*

Waiting for the End — *for Isela Vega in memory of Warren + Sam.*

1984: Knockin' at Your Door — *para La Beta y La Esmeralda.*

Please Don't Bury Me Alive — *for Tomás Rivera.*
The "home is..." line is from Robert Frost's "The Death of A Hired Man."

ABOUT THE AUTHOR

Playwright and poet Gregg Barrios comes to the arts after a successful career as a journalist for the *Los Angeles Times*, a book editor for the *San Antonio Express-News*, an editorial page editor for *Rumbo*, a Spanish language daily, and a teacher in Texas.

As a published poet, Barrios has three books to his credit including *Puro Rollo, The Air-Conditioned Apollo*, and *Healthy Self*.

His poetry has appeared in publications ranging from *Hecho en Tejas*, an anthology of Tejano literature, Latina magazine, and the UCLA anthology, *Aztlán and Vietnam*. More recently, his poem "Chale Guerra" was the only Latino contribution to the anthology *Home Front: An America at War Reader* (Free Press).

Barrios received a commission and grant through the Ford Foundation Gateway Program at the Guadalupe Cultural Arts Center in San Antonio to research and develop *Rancho Pancho*. *Rancho Pancho* received its first full production in 2008 at Jump-Start. The play was performed at the Tennessee Williams Theater Festival in Provincetown. The play was selected by the *San Antonio Express-News* as one of the top ten productions in 2008. The play was published in June 2009. A production premiered in Phoenix, Arizona in 2010.

The *San Antonio Express-News* selected Barrios as one of NINE in '09 San Antonio artists and writers on the verge of a national breakthrough.

Barrios is a Texas native and a resident of San Antonio. He is a member of the Dramatists' Guild and on the Board of Directors of the National Book Critics Circle.